AF440517

WHO IS MARTHA STEWART?

CELEBRITY BIOGRAPHY BOOKS

Children's Biography Books

Speedy Publishing LLC
40 E. Main St. #1156
Newark, DE 19711
www.speedypublishing.com

Copyright © 2017

All Rights reserved. No part of this book may be reproduced or used in any way or form or by any means whether electronic or mechanical, this means that you cannot record or photocopy any material ideas or tips that are provided in this book.

n this book, we're going to talk about the interesting life of businesswoman Martha Stewart. So, let's get right to it!

PAPER

Decorative boxes from Martha Stewart's collections.

WHO IS MARTHA STEWART?

M artha Stewart is a dynamic businesswoman, writer, television personality, and lifestyle guru. She's created a brand around her name that combines interior design, do-it-yourself crafts, and gourmet home cooking.

Martha's birth name was Martha Kostyra and she was born in New Jersey in 1941. Her dad was a salesman in the pharmaceutical industry and her mother taught and took care of their home. There were six children in the Kostyra family and Martha was the second of the six. Her parents were proud of their Polish heritage and the children learned about the history and culture of their homeland.

Martha Stewart.

M artha's family moved to the middle class town of Nutley, New Jersey when Martha was just a toddler. Their household was organized and the children were all expected to pitch in and do their part. As she got older, Martha was schooled by her mother who taught her how to prepare delicious meals and how to be clever with a sewing machine.

Martha helped her dad with the gardening in their yard. At least once every year, Martha had the opportunity to visit with her grandparents and she and her grandmother used to put up preserves together. All these activities were to blend together and provide a foundation for Martha's later career.

MARTHA STEWART'S
COOKING SCHOOL

While in high school, Martha made money by holding parties for children as well as babysitting. She also did fashion modeling starting at the age of 13 and continuing through her college years. She made a good income to help pay for her schooling.

One of her clients was the perfume company Chanel. She enrolled in Barnard College in New York. She started her studies in European history and then graduated in 1962 with a double major in History and Architectural History.

Chanel shop in old Marais quarter.

BARNARD

While she was in college, she met a law student who was attending Yale. His name was Andy Stewart. They got married in 1961 and she took Andy's last name—Stewart.

She and Andy did some traveling and Martha continued to do some modeling until she became pregnant with her daughter Alexis who was born in 1965. When Alexis was two years old, Martha decided she wanted to go back to work.

Martha Stewart at The Breast Cancer Research Foundation Annual Spring Gala.

Encouraged by her father-in-law, Martha studied for the securities exam and passed. She interviewed for a position at the three-year-old financial firm of Monness, Williams, and Sidel and got the job. She was a highly successful stockbroker for six years.

M artha and her husband bought a 19th century farmhouse in Connecticut in 1971. They called their home Turkey Hill and Martha decided to quit working at the financial firm so she could devote more time to restoring the house. She was always interested in cooking and when she had been working as a stockbroker she had had little time to prepare meals for her husband and daughter. She was always looking for creative ways to do quick grocery shopping after work and put a great meal on the table.

WGBH-TV
SERIES
THE FRENCH CHEF

Now that she was home, she had more time to focus on cooking and she self-taught by studying Julia Child's famous book, *Mastering the Art of French Cooking.* In 1973, she decided to challenge herself once again by starting a catering business.

Martha's unique style of gourmet food coupled with a beautiful, artistic presentation gained her a fan base of influential clients in the corporate and celebrity worlds. Within 10 years she built her business, Martha Stewart, Inc., to earnings of more than $1 million dollars annually.

MARTHA STEWART™
LIVING
CABINETS, COUNTERTOPS AND HARDWARE

PUBLISHING SUCCESS

Martha was always meeting celebrities and corporate executives during her catering events. At a party where she was catering hostess for a book her husband was launching, she met an influential book publisher, Alan Mirken. He was the head of the Crown Publishing Group. Mirken was very impressed with Martha and encouraged her to create a book.

Martha's magazine.

Martha worked with a ghostwriter to produce her very first book called *Entertaining,* which was published in 1982. It was a huge success and Martha soon put out a string of other books about quick cooking, appetizers, pies and tarts, planning for weddings, and celebrating at Christmas. The decade of the 1980s was filled with publishing profits for Martha.

FROM
AMERICAN
PICKERS
Nov / Dec 2013
NEW
Well Styled Home
Merry & Bright
72 TIPS FOR VINTAGE
1ST
Flea Market Déc
Country Sampler
DECORATING IDEAS & WHERE TO BUY COUNTRY ACCESSORIES
Homespun
VINT
FI
Ideas and
fall
Ideas a
fall
v
YEAR'S
MARTHA STEWART
Living
THANKSGIVING
101
PAGE 114
NEW SECRETS FOR
golden,
crispy turkey

While she was working on these publications, she also authored dozens of newspaper columns and magazine articles. Martha was already well known, but her appearances on Oprah Winfrey's and Larry King's television shows boosted her into celebrity status.

Woman flipping through magazine.

While her career was in full bloom, her personal life began to crumble. After she was separated from her husband for three years, they divorced in 1990 after 29 years of marriage.

MARTHA STEWART
MARTHA STEWART
COLLECTION

MARTHA STEWART LIVING

Stewart's next major venture was a magazine business. She signed a contract with Time Publishing Ventures to create her own magazine called *Martha Stewart Living.* The first issue of the magazine was released in 1990 and today the magazine's circulation is over 2 million copies. Martha then expanded the interest in the magazine to a television program beginning in 1993 as a 30-minute program.

Martha Stewart Collection.

MART

MARTHA STEWART

The program was so popular that it was expanded to airing every weekday for 30 minutes. By 1999, it was a full-hour show with

VING RADIO

30-minute shows on the weekends. Martha was also making regular appearances on the *Today Show* on NBC and the *Early Show* on CBS.

Martha Stewart Living Radio logo.

MARTHA
STEWART

MARTHA STEWART LIVING OMNIMEDIA

Along with her business partner, Sharon Patrick, Martha decided to purchase all of her print, merchandise, and TV businesses and put them under one roof so that she could control her own brand name and intellectual property. Her name *"Martha Stewart"* was a brand name that was worth millions of dollars. She and Sharon Patrick created the company *Martha Stewart Living Omnimedia.*

Martha Stewart Living Omnimedia logo.

Martha was Chief Executive Officer (CEO) of the new company and Sharon Patrick was Chief Operations Officer (COO). They soon launched a website to go with the Martha Stewart Living magazine as well as a catalog business and a business selling floral arrangements directly to consumers.

MARTHA STEWART'S
COOKING SCHOOL
Lessons and Recipes for the Home Cook

macy's

n 1999, the company went public and the price of the stock went from $18 a share to $38 a share. Martha Stewart's wealth was now estimated to about $1 billion dollars. She was the first self-made woman billionaire in America. In addition to the selling she was doing with her own company, Martha's products were also being sold in other popular retail chains and department stores like Home Depot and Macys.

Martha was at the very height of her career as a businesswoman when she made a mistake that cost her dearly. She had joined the board of directors of the NYSE, which stands for New York Stock Exchange, just four months before the scandal happened. She owned stock in a company called ImClone Systems, which was creating a new drug to be used by cancer patients.

The New york Stock Exchange in New York, NY.

Supposedly, she was given information that the Food And Drug Administration was not going to approve ImClone's new drug. She sold hundreds of shares of stock she had before the announcement was made, to save herself stock market losses. This type of information that someone receives ahead of the public regarding a stock and the action taken to unload stocks is called *"insider trading."*

M artha pleaded innocent to the charges, but she was convicted and sent to prison for 5

Newspaper with the breaking news.

months before she served the rest of her sentence under house arrest. She was also fined $30,000.

The reaction to Martha going to jail was mixed. Some people thought she was innocent. Others thought that she deserved to be sentenced for thinking she was so powerful that she was **"above the law."** Still others thought that people in powerful positions were bringing her down because she was such a successful woman. In any case, Stewart's companies continued to make profits while she was in prison.

It seemed that Martha's brand would be forever tarnished by her prison record, but Martha kept going after she got out of prison in March of 2005. The television network NBC made her the star of two new television shows. One was a daytime program where she would show the audience how to do her crafts and foods. The other program was a spinoff of the show called The Apprentice that was produced by famed television producer Mark Burnett and billionaire businessman, now president, Donald Trump.

Entrepreneur Martha Stewart sat down with
Jeff Morey for a one-on-one interview keynote
at the 2014 IGC Show.

Although the Apprentice spinoff didn't attract enough viewers, her how-to program did well. Martha continued to grow Martha Stewart Omnimedia, Inc. and sold it to a company called Sequential Brands for $353 million dollars in 2015. At its height, the company was worth $2 billion dollars. Martha will continue to be associated with all the diverse brands that she created.

Awesome! Now you know more about the life and achievements of Martha Stewart. You can find more Biography books from Baby Professor by searching the website of your favorite book retailer.

Martha Stewart's
COOKIES
ake and to share
MARTHA
STEWART'S
WEDDING
CAKES
MORE THAN 100 INS   CAKES
AN INDISPENSABLE GUIDE FOR   AND THE BAKER
MARTHA STEW
WENDY KROMER

Visit
BABY PROFESSOR
EDUCATION KIDS
www.BabyProfessorBooks.com
to download Free Baby Professor eBooks
and view our catalog of new and exciting
Children's Books

www.ingramcontent.com/pod-product-compliance
Lightning Source LLC
Chambersburg PA
CBHW080806120726
48001CB00009B/2865